BEARS OF LITTLE TICKING

LIBRA *(September 23rd–October 22nd)*

vember 21st)

SAGITTARIUS *(November 22nd–December 21st)*

CAPRICORN *(December 22nd–January 19th)*

AQUARIUS *(January 20th–February 18th)*

PISCES *(February 19th–March 20th)*

Dedication

This book and all others in
the series are dedicated to
the memories we cherish of
our dear departed friend

Peter Bull

House of Nisbet Ltd
Winscombe, England

Typeset, printed and produced by DDS Colour Printers
Unit 10, Worle Industrial Centre, Weston-super-Mare, England. Tel: (0934) 516902

TUNBRIDGE

THE BARGE BEAR

PAULINE McMILLAN

Nisbet "Zodiac Bears" Series

House of Nisbet Ltd., Winscombe, England

ISBN 0 948045 10 8

Most of the bears of Little Ticking village live in ordinary houses or cottages. However, Julius, the Head Bear, has his house up a tree and Nipper has a caravan under a hedgerow. But the most unusual home of all belongs to Tunbridge.

He is the bear who looks after the village wells, water tanks, pipes and taps. He loves Anything To Do With Water. He is so fond of it that he lives right on top of it, in a barge on the River Tick. He also likes painting and has decorated his barge, which is called 'Daffodil', with lots of bright patterns. Some of the other river animals have done the same, and their boats are a cheerful sight as they pass by.

Early one morning Tunbridge sat on the river bank re-painting his tin jugs and buckets. He wanted everything on his barge to look spick and span because today was rather special. He had promised to take his friends, the other Zodiac bears, on a river picnic aboard 'Daffodil'.

Although 'Daffodil' does have an engine he only uses it for going on long trips. For picnics he thinks it is more enjoyable and much quieter to use a barge horse who walks along the tow-path beside the river, pulling the boat after him on the end of a rope.

DAFFO
OF
LITTLE TIC

After making sure that all was tidy, Tunbridge went to the stable to fetch Podge, the village pony, who was going to be barge horse for the day. As they passed her cottage Doris came out with something in her paw.

'I've made this crochet-work hat for Podge,' she said, 'It will stop the flies biting his ears.'

As Tunbridge put the hat on him Podge gave a conceited grin.

'How Terribly Attractive this will make me look,' he thought to himself (for he is Inclined To Vanity).

Soon all the other bears appeared at their gates with bags and picnic baskets.

Laughing and chatting, everyone followed Tunbridge down the lane towards the river.

'It's a perfect day for an outing,' said Plumby, 'Just feel that warm sun on your fur.'

'Yes,' agreed Tunbridge, 'I thought we'd go down as far as the village of Deeping Slumber to have lunch.'

'Couldn't be better!' cried Baity, 'It's a wonderful spot for fishing.'

'Do you EVER think of anything else?' sighed Doris, his wife.

But when the bears reached the river a nasty shock awaited them. 'Daffodil' had gone! They gazed into the distance but could see nothing on the water besides ducks and swans.

'Daffodil' must have broken loose from her moorings,' said Tunbridge, 'I don't understand why that has happened.

I'm always careful to tie her up securely.'

The bears dumped their baskets in the shade of a tree then split up into small groups. They went in different directions along the river bank to search for the missing boat.

Although they walked a mile both ways from the spot where 'Daffodil' had been, there was no sign of her. Tunbridge looked very worried.

'I don't think she floated off by accident,' he said, 'I think someone has stolen her!'

'Don't worry. We'll help you get her back,' said the other bears, patting him to cheer him up.

The picnic was forgotten as some of them returned to the village to fetch their bicycles so they could ride further along the river bank in search of 'Daffodil'.

Meanwhile Tunbridge and his two best friends, Bruin and Baity, rode Podge in the opposite direction keeping a look-out for the lost barge.

There were many boats on the river and some of them were barges, but the bears could not see 'Daffodil' among them. All the other boat owners knew Tunbridge, and he told them what had happened. None of them had seen his barge in the area, but they promised to watch for her on the river.

At last the bears reached Deeping Slumber and rested for a while at the inn. Jocky Scott, the landlord, was a good friend but when they told him their story he shook his head.

'Tunbridge and 'Daffodil' are a well-known sight on this river,' he said, 'I'd have spotted her at once if anyone had tried to take her past. I definitely haven't seen her today.'

'It's a mystery,' said Tunbridge unhappily, 'She seems to have vanished into thin air. But how could anyone take something so big without folk noticing?'

Jocky brought mugs of nettle beer, and as they drank he rubbed his chin thoughtfully.

'I've just remembered something,' he said, 'A bit further on from here a stretch of the old canal joins the river. It's not much used nowadays and would be the sort of place where a stolen boat might be hidden.'

THE
BOAT
INN

Jocky explained that the old canal path was rather tangled and it would be easier to explore by boat. So the bears left Podge in the field behind the inn and Jocky loaned them his dinghy.

They rowed down the canal, staring hard at some barges moored there but none of them was 'Daffodil'.

'Oh, yummy!' said Baity suddenly, 'A bush covered in ripe blackberries above our heads!'

'Do be careful!' cried Tunbridge as his friend stood up in the boat, reaching for the fruit.

But he spoke too late, for next second, 'SPLOSH!', Baity had toppled into the water.

Luckily all the Zodiac bears have learned to swim so Baity swam to the canal bank and clung on to a tree root.

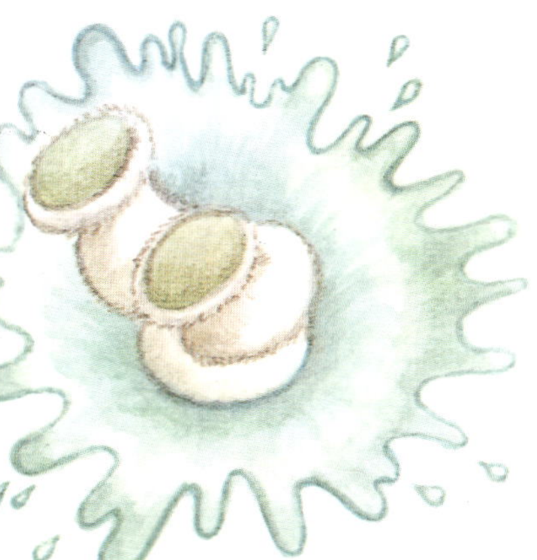

The others rowed across and pulled him back into the dinghy as he apologised.

'That was awfully stupid of me,' he gasped, shaking the water from his ears, 'I should have remembered you always stay sitting in a rowing boat except when you climb in and out.'

Tunbridge was staring at the tree Baity had been clinging to. It was a willow, its long, slender branches hanging low like a leafy curtain over the canal bank.

'Look,' he said as he pulled some leaves aside. 'There's another channel of water behind here. We'd never have noticed it if you hadn't fallen in.'

They glided into the hidden waterway between high old walls and banks crowded with strange plants. It was so overgrown and mysterious it was like moving through a glittering green tunnel.

They came to a patch of sunlight and moored the dinghy for Baity to dry himself. Bruin sat on the grass and kept peering towards the dark shadows on the opposite bank. Suddenly he gave a shout of excitement and pointed at something under the trees.

'There she is! There's "Daffodil!"'

Tunbridge stared at the barge which was nearly covered by overhanging willows.

'But my boat is painted in all sorts of colours. That one is a muddy green.'

Yet when they crossed over for a closer look, Tunbridge recognised the fancy brasses on the chimney and realised it was indeed his own boat.

The bears jumped on board the barge and threw open the hatch to look down into the cabin. They were amazed at what they saw, for there sat a family of weasels, eating lunch at Tunbridge's table.

The mother and the little weasels looked scared but the fierce father jumped up angrily.

'Get out of here!' he snarled at the bears.

'I'll do no such thing!' cried Tunbridge, 'This is MY boat and those are my cups and plates you're using!'

The father weasel sprang at the bears, punching at them with his paws and next second a Terrible Scuffle was taking place on the river bank. All the little weasels rushed up on deck to watch.

'Pop! Pop! Oh, Pop!' they wailed in frightened voices, 'Please, Mr. Bear, don't hurt our poor Pop!'

Teddy bears never like to hurt anyone, but the father weasel was in such a fury he had to be Restrained. Somehow Tunbridge, Bruin and Baity ended up sitting on him to hold him down while he growled and bared his sharp teeth at them.

'Now stop this nonsense!' said Bruin firmly, 'There are three of us to one of you. But we'll let you get up if you promise to behave.'

The weasel suddenly went quiet and stopped struggling. The bears let go of him, rather warily, but the fight seemed to have gone out of him. He slumped down on a nearby stone, his chin in his paws.

'Well, what have you got to say for yourself?' frowned Tunbridge.

'It was a rotten thing to do, stealing our friend's boat,' added Baity, 'It's his home, you know.'

The weasel's shoulders drooped and he gave a deep, miserable sigh.

'I suppose I should have known we wouldn't get away with it,' he mumbled, 'But we're Desperate — '

'Desperate! Desperate!' wailed the little weasels, 'That's what we are, Mr. Bear, Desperate!'

'Look, I think you'd better explain what this is all about,' said Tunbridge in a more kindly tone.

The weasel, whose name was Billy Musty, explained that he had worked on a farm. The cottage he and his family had lived in belonged to the farmer and went with his job.

But then the farm was sold to some animals who were going to build a factory on the land. Billy lost his job and the weasel family had to leave their cottage which the new owners were going to knock down.

'I've tried and tried but I can't get another job,' said Billy, 'We've wandered from village to village trying to find work and a place to live. We've camped out in woods and dry ditches. It's been hard on the wife and little 'uns.'

Then he explained how they had come to Little Ticking that morning and seen 'Daffodil' moored on the river.

'I never meant to steal her, not at first,' he said, 'We just meant to ask the owner if we could have a cup of tea.'

'Then when I saw there was nobody on board I had this crazy idea,' he went on, 'You see, it was such a cosy home, I thought if only we could sort of BORROW it, it would be a safe place for the family to stay while I travelled round looking for work. I thought that whoever it belonged to couldn't be as Desperate as us!'

'Awful Desperate, Mr. Bear!' squeaked the little weasels.

Billy Musty had found some of Tunbridge's paints and mixed them together into the muddy green. He had disguised 'Daffodil' so folk along the river wouldn't recognise her as she passed, then he had hidden her in the secret backwater.

'I realise now it was a bad thing to do. I'm very sorry,' he said, looking ashamed.

'Very, very sorry,' echoed the little weasels, 'Please don't give our Pop to a policedog, Mr. Bear!'

The bears drew aside to talk things over.

'I can't just throw them off the barge,' whispered Tunbridge, 'They've got no money and nowhere to go.'

'Yet without 'Daffodil' you won't have a home yourself,' Bruin reminded him, 'Although you're welcome to live with any of us, you know you wouldn't like living on dry land.'

In the end they decided to take the weasels back to Little Ticking to Sort Things Out. Tunbridge told Julius and the others what had happened, and the Head Bear said he was to bring Billy Musty to a meeting of all the bears.

'Stealing is a Very Serious Crime, you know,' said Julius looking severely through his specs at Billy, who looked sad and dejected.

'But he did have Good Reasons for what he did,' added Nipper, a gentle-natured bear.

'It's still Wrong though,' said Polly Hester, 'Folk who do Wrong should be Punished.'

'I think it must be enough of a Punishment having nowhere to live,' said Doris, thinking how she would miss her own dear cottage if she had to leave it.

'I do want to make amends for what I did,' said Billy, 'Please gentlebears, let me re-paint Mr. Tunbridge's boat, dig your gardens or do something to show I'm sorry.'

'Amends . . . mend . . . mending things,' muttered Tunbridge to himself. Suddenly he looked up. 'I've got it!' he cried.

The others stared at him but couldn't see anything.

'Where is It?' asked Saxon.

'On the river bank, just past the bridge,' he answered.

'What is?' they all asked, puzzled.

'A ruined cottage!' shouted Tunbridge, 'I've often seen it but never really thought about it until now. We'll help Billy to fix it up and he can live there!'

Everyone went to look at the cottage which had been empty for years and years, and was in a bad state. The roof had fallen in and a tree was growing through it. All the floorboards and the window-frames had rotted and the doors were gone.

'Ooh, it's awfully SPOOKY,' said Polly Hester with a shiver.

Grass and weeds grew in all the rooms and there was a damp, creepy sort of smell everywhere.

'Hmm, a great deal needs to be done,' said Tunbridge, 'But if we all lend a paw with the work it won't take too long.'

'In a few weeks this will be a different house,' nodded Bruin. He was very clever at Do-It-Yourself and knew about such things.

He was right. Everyone in Little Ticking helped in some way. The tree inside the cottage was cut down and the dark, tangled garden was cleared and dug. New paths were laid, the roof was mended and the floors were renewed.

All day long the river bank echoed to the sound of hammering, sawing and the scrape of folk mixing cement. Billy Musty worked hardest of all and whistled to himself with happiness.

The Little weasels made themselves very useful and popped up everywhere to fetch and carry things for the workers.

CEMEN
BUTTERCUP
YELLOW

While the cottage was being fixed the weasel family stayed on board 'Daffodil' with Tunbridge. It felt very cramped, but it was the noise that really bothered him. The little weasels sang and shouted to each other at the tops of their voices, and the baby had a squeaky little cry that made Tunbridge put his paws over his ears. He was glad when their place was ready for them to move in.

The Mustys had nothing to put in their new house but that problem was soon solved. Each bear and animal brought them something from his or her own home.

Bruin made the weasels a set of chairs and a table, Julius sent two armchairs and a rug, and Doris brought them sheets and blankets. Plumby, who runs the Village Shop, sent a box

of groceries, enough to stock their larder for a month. Gordon Blue, the bear who is an expert cook, gave them a good set of pots and pans, and Bella Plush (who is very rich) sent a money box full of money.

Tunbridge decorated some jugs and buckets for them, like the ones on his barge, and he also painted a cradle which Bruin had made for the baby.

'How can I ever repay your kindness?' Billy Musty asked Tunbridge, 'You and the others have gone to all this trouble for strangers who stole your boat.'

'You aren't strangers. You're our neighbours now,' smiled Tunbridge, 'Part of the village of Little Ticking.'

Soon afterwards Tunbridge heard of a boat-builder

further down the river who was looking for an assistant. Tunbridge told Billy who got the job and found that he liked boat-building better than farm work.

As for 'Daffodil', Tunbridge enjoyed himself re-painting her lovely patterns all over again. Last of all he proudly added her name, 'Daffodil Of Little Ticking.'

And in her cottage Mrs. Musty did some pawcraft of her own. She made patch cushions, quilts and rag rugs to brighten the weasels' new home. But she took the greatest care of all in stitching a beautiful motto to hang over the fireplace. It said,

'BLESS ALL TEDDY BEARS'.

If you have enjoyed meeting "your" Zodiac Bear through the pages of this book, you may wish to know that all of The Zodiac Bears are now available as 14″ jointed bears handmade by House of Nisbet in the traditional way and dressed as they appear in the book. Ask for your Nisbet Zodiac Bear at fine toy and department stores throughout the world.

THE ZODIAC BIRTHDAY

ARIES *(March 21st–April 20th)*

TAURUS *(April 21st–May 20th)*

GEMINI *(May 21st–June 20th)*

CANCER *(June 21st–July 22nd)*

LEO *(July 23rd–August 22nd)*

VIRGO *(August 23rd–September 22nd)*